FROM THE BIBLE-TEACHING MINISTRY OF
CHARLES R. SWINDOLL

The
SECRET
to Facing Hard Days

Insight on Discouragement, Guilt, and Anxiety

INSIGHT FOR LIVING

THE SECRET TO FACING HARD DAYS
Insight on Discouragement, Guilt, and Anxiety
From the Bible-Teaching Ministry of Charles R. Swindoll

Charles R. Swindoll has devoted his life to the clear, practical teaching and application of God's Word and His grace. A pastor at heart, Chuck has served as senior pastor to congregations in Texas, Massachusetts, and California. He currently pastors Stonebriar Community Church in Frisco, Texas, but Chuck's listening audience extends far beyond a local church body. As a leading program in Christian broadcasting, *Insight for Living* airs in major Christian radio markets around the world, reaching people groups in languages they can understand. Chuck's extensive writing ministry has also served the body of Christ worldwide and his leadership as president and now chancellor of Dallas Theological Seminary has helped prepare and equip a new generation for ministry. Chuck and Cynthia, his partner in life and ministry, have four grown children and ten grandchildren.

Editor in Chief: Cynthia Swindoll, President, Insight for Living
Executive Vice President: Wayne Stiles, Th.M., D.Min., Dallas Theological Seminary
Writer: Barb Peil, M.A., Christian Education, Dallas Theological Seminary
Theological Editor: John Adair, Th.M., Ph.D., Dallas Theological Seminary
Content Editor: Amy L. Snedaker, B.A., English, Rhodes College
Copy Editors: Jim Craft, M.A., English, Mississippi College
      Kathryn Merritt, M.A., English, Hardin-Simmons University
Project Coordinator, Creative Ministries: Melanie Munnell, M.A., Humanities,
      The University of Texas at Dallas
Project Coordinator, Communications: Sarah Magnoni, A.A.S., University of Wisconsin
Proofreader: Paula McCoy, B.A., English, Texas A&M University-Commerce
Designer: Margaret Gulliford, B.A., Graphic Design, Taylor University
Production Artist: Nancy Gustine, B.F.A., Advertising Art, University of North Texas

Published By:
IFL Publishing House
A Division of Insight for Living
Post Office Box 251007
Plano, Texas 75025-1007

ISBN: 978-1-57972-915-8
Printed in the United States of America

TABLE OF CONTENTS

A NOTE FROM
Chuck Swindoll

Dear Friend:

I know something about you. You don't read something titled *The Secret to Facing Hard Days* just for fun. You face hard days and so do I. Perhaps you're facing some right now.

I don't know of anything that will take the wind out of your sails like discouragement. And who hasn't known a restless night filled with worries about tomorrow? And when those pesky, thorny doubts about God's forgiveness get stuck under your skin, you need relief from guilt that only a Savior can provide.

Good thing we have one. We have an ever-present Savior. His name is Jesus. He stands beside us. Even better, He takes the lead at life's most critical moments . . . and His mercy makes all the difference.

You have nothing to fear. You really don't. There's help available from the God who loves you when you face hard days. His Word offers perspective and correction. When we are swamped by the ever-rising tide of discouragement, He brings relief. When doubts invade our spirits, He grants deliverance through the path of truth. When dark moments leave us feeling fearful, believing that things will never change, He guides us toward a way of escape. The Lord offers us hope beyond the questions of today. He gives strength for the weakest times. And when we release our burdens to Him, His relief floods our lives in unexpected moments.

As our staff gathered together around this volume you hold in your hands, our prayer was that the Lord would lift your spirit by transforming your mind. We asked that He would strengthen you to see the value of dwelling on things that are true, honest, just, pure, lovely, and of good report. Our prayer is that you would take the burden of discouragement or guilt or fear that you find yourself consumed with today and trade all that anxiety for hope, finding in that process great peace and lasting relief.

Today, as you turn to God deliberately and confidently, may you be reminded that Christ loves you and keeps on loving you even during the hard days.

Chuck Swindoll

Charles R. Swindoll

And now to him who can keep you on your feet, standing tall in his bright presence, fresh and celebrating—to our one God, our only Savior, through Jesus Christ, our Master, be glory, majesty, strength, and rule before all time, and now, and to the end of all time. Yes.
—Jude 1:24–25 MSG

The
SECRET
to Facing Hard Days

Insight on Discouragement, Guilt, and Anxiety

DISCOURAGEMENT
Getting to the Other Side

Discouragement is part of the natural roller coaster of life; all of us are susceptible to circumstances that weaken our spirits. During different seasons of our lives, most of us will experience in varying intensities a loss of hope, due to circumstances that are sometimes within and sometimes outside our control. We may feel defeated, exhausted, or "under a cloud."

What's a Christian to do? Deny emotions? Claim God's promises? Hold on tight and ride out the storm? How do we get through the down days? How do we keep discouragement from spiraling into depression? The answers are not always clear.

Discouragement is too complicated to solve with a single, simple solution. Entire libraries have been devoted to the causes and treatments of depression, discouragement, and suffering. In this chapter, we will focus on what the Bible says about discouragement and how followers of Christ can increase in wisdom through life's daily, relentless challenges and emerge with greater confidence in the work of God in our lives. The conclusion of this very personal journey is, like everything else, grounded and secure in the person and work of Jesus Christ. Our lives are "hidden" in His life (Colossians 3:3). And His promised presence, especially on difficult days, provides the strength we need to keep trusting Him.

The First Response to Discouragement

Discouragement dims our perspective of how God is working in the overall plan of our lives.

When days of discouragement surface, you can choose to see them first as evidence of God's wanting your attention. Your best response, whatever the cause, is to open yourself to *whatever* the Lord has for you. If you're facing discouragement and this is your attitude, God will use this experience for good in your life. You may want to rationalize, argue, ignore, or shout against discouragement, but admit, if only by faith, that God is at work.

1

God is accomplishing His purposes in this raw season in your life. He may be using this pain as a warning signal of something that's gone wrong in your relationship with Him. He may want you to face something difficult, like an area in which you need to trust Him or a sinful pattern you need to cut from your life. He could be growing you up, using difficult circumstances to mature you. Or He may just be removing all other distractions so He can help you learn to respond to Him.

Whatever His purpose, you can believe by faith, from the start, that God will not waste your pain. Whether He has engineered the circumstances or sin has brought on this discouragement, He can redeem this season and turn it into a gift.

Scripture OFFERS MANY *purposes* BEHIND OUR *difficult days.*

We suffer:

so that God may *teach us endurance* (James 1:3)

so that God may *bring us to repentance* (Hebrews 12:5–11)

so that we might *comfort and encourage others* (2 Corinthians 1:3–6)

so that we may *glorify God* (John 9:1–3; 1 Peter 4:16)

so that we may *share in Christ's suffering* (Philippians 3:8–10)

so that we may *be strengthened* (1 Peter 5:10)

so that others will *be saved* (2 Timothy 2:8–10)

to conform us to *Christ's image* (Romans 8:28–29)

to move others to *comfort and pray for us* (2 Corinthians 1:8–11)

to keep us *humble* (2 Corinthians 12:7)

to motivate us to *go to God for help* (Psalm 30:6–8)

to enjoy the *nearness of God's presence* (James 4:6–8)

In the Bible, God gives realistic portraits of people who faced struggles just like ours. You'll likely recognize these well-known and well-respected leaders in Israel's history and appreciate the Bible's practical presentation of the varied factors that played a role in their discouragement.

Elijah

He ran from Jezebel after the victory on Mount Carmel (1 Kings 19).

PHYSICALLY: Elijah was exhausted. His adrenaline pumped so hard for so long that all his energy was depleted.

EMOTIONALLY: Elijah feared for his life. Jezebel's threats shredded his faith.

SPIRITUALLY: Elijah's negative emotions overshadowed his faith in God. Elijah forgot all the miracles God had done in his recent dealings in spiritual warfare. He doubted God.

Jonah

He wanted to die after the salvation of Nineveh (Jonah 4).

PHYSICALLY: Jonah experienced several exhausting weeks, including his ride in the fish and the days of fervent preaching.

EMOTIONALLY: Jonah was torn between the need to obey God and his own resentment of God's concern for such heathen people. Jonah's sense of superiority over the people of Nineveh ate him up.

SPIRITUALLY: Jonah was angry at God for showing mercy to Nineveh.

David

He hid in the wilderness from murderous Saul (Psalm 69).

PHYSICALLY: David's body ached from running and scrounging for food and shelter.

EMOTIONALLY: David described himself as drowning. He felt utter despair for his life.

SPIRITUALLY: David waited on God for deliverance and pleaded with God for answers and rescue.

Can You Relate?

A Man Just Like Us—
Lessons from Elijah

James 5:17 says it simply: "Elijah was a man just like us" (NIV). Elijah, God's great Old Testament prophet, suffered from discouragement after his victory over wicked Queen Jezebel at Mount Carmel. How could Elijah have felt down after a victory like that? Let's look at the contributing causes.

Read 1 Kings 19:1–8.

1 ELIJAH WASN'T *thinking clearly.*

As Elijah collapsed under the juniper tree, he failed to consider the source of his discouragement. It hadn't come from God but from wicked Jezebel. He was wallowing in the wash of his emotions rather than examining them for accuracy. Fear is behind more discouragement than we'd like to admit. Fear of criticism (*What will they think?*); fear of responsibility (*What if I can't handle this?*); and fear of failure (*What if I blow it?*) can cause a major onset of the blues.

2 ELIJAH *separated himself* FROM STRENGTHENING RELATIONSHIPS.

First Kings 19:3 concludes, Elijah "left his servant." Lonely people are discouraged people. One of the best things Elijah could have done was to seek out someone who could bring him strength and objectivity. But it's interesting how human nature works. When we get discouraged, the first thing we tend to do is to get alone—often the worst thing we can do.

3 ELIJAH WAS CAUGHT IN THE *emotional slump* THAT FOLLOWS A GREAT VICTORY.

It's baffling that victory can sometimes feel like failure, but it's true. Often, our most vulnerable moments come after tremendous efforts or big successes.

4 ELIJAH WAS *physically exhausted* AND *emotionally spent.*

Fatigue brings great vulnerability. When physically or emotionally exhausted, we're prime candidates for discouragement. Our defenses are lowered, and things can seem bleaker than they really are. Weariness often occurs after a victory or when we're halfway through major projects.

5 ELIJAH SUBMITTED TO *self-pity*.

Self-pity will lie every time. It will exaggerate. It may lead us to tears. It even took Elijah to the point of contemplating suicide: "I have had enough, LORD . . . take my life" (1 Kings 19:4 NIV).

So Elijah, follower of God, heroic servant . . . sat alone in a cave. How did God treat His discouraged servant? Did He tell Elijah, "Get a grip, buddy"? Did He shame him—"Where's your faith, Elijah?" No. Consistent with His tenderness for people who are hurting, God modeled kindness to discouraged Elijah:

1. God gave him rest and refreshment (19:5–8).

2. God spoke to him gently (19:9–18).

3. God reassured him of his continued purpose (19:15–18).

4. God provided him with a friend who would minister to him (19:19, 21).

God was, in effect, telling Elijah, "You're still important! You're not perfect, but you're still My choice."

Brothers, as an example of patience
in the face of suffering, take the prophets
who spoke in the name of the Lord. As you know,
we consider blessed those who have persevered.
You have heard of Job's perseverance and
have seen what the Lord finally brought about.
The Lord is full of compassion and mercy.
(James 5:10–11 NIV)

A Hope Transplant

by Charles R. Swindoll

One of the greatest benefits to be gleaned from the Bible is perspective. When we get discouraged, we temporarily lose our perspective. Little things become mammoth. A slight irritation, like a pebble in a shoe, seems huge. Motivation is drained away and, worst of all, hope departs.

God's Word is tailor-made for gray-slush days. It sends a beam of light through the fog. It signals safety when we fear we'll never make it through. Such big-picture perspective gives us a hope transplant, and within a brief period of time, we have escaped the bleak and boring and we're back at soaring.

There is a magnificent thought nestled in the fifteenth chapter of Romans that promises all this.

> *For whatever was written in earlier times was written for our instruction, so that through perseverance and the encouragement of the Scriptures we might have hope. (Romans 15:4)*

God has not designed a life of despondency for us. He wants His people to have hope. Through endurance and through encouragement from the Scriptures, we can gain hope. You may say, "I don't have much endurance. Furthermore, I feel terribly discouraged." Read the next verse. It is written for everyone who feels that way.

> *Now may the God who gives perseverance and encouragement grant you to be of the same mind with one another according to Christ Jesus. (15:5)*

God wants to give us both perseverance and encouragement. He says, in effect, "If you will submit yourself to the teaching of My Word, I will give you 'perseverance' (the word literally means 'endurance'—that ability to hang in there) and 'encouragement'—a lifting up of your spirits." He will replace discouragement with fresh hope. And, ultimately, why?

> *So that with one accord you may with one voice glorify the God and Father of our Lord Jesus Christ. (15:6)*

What a priceless nugget of truth there is in these three verses! What I find here is the scriptural basis for encouragement. God offers instruction, but then it's our move. We must *accept* His instruction and *apply* it to our lives. Then, and only then, can we expect to cash in on the benefits of His instruction. So you see, application is the essential link between instruction and change. God promises us hope—relief from discouragement. Yes, it's available. And we can actually stand strong through discouraging times . . . but only if we apply His instructions.

As hard as it may be for you to believe, you will be able to walk right through those gray-slush days with confidence. The One who gives perseverance and encouragement will escort you through the down days, never leaving you in the lurch. Discouragement may be awful, but it is not terminal. You will soar again.[1]

Ten SCRIPTURES to PRAY When You're *Feeling Discouraged*

You have incredible power available to you when you pray God's Word back to Him. Personalize the following verses as you talk to God. For example, with the first verse, you might pray something like this:

> *Lord, You told me to not be anxious about anything, but in everything, by prayer and supplication and with thanksgiving, to present my requests to You. Lord, I am thankful for this invitation from You. I am thankful for the way You've provided for me in the past. Now, Lord, here is my need today. Please help me with _____.*

1. Pray instead of worry.

Be anxious for nothing, but in everything by prayer and supplication with thanksgiving let your requests be made known to God. (Philippians 4:6)

2. Remember God is with you.

"Be strong and courageous, do not be afraid or tremble at them, for the LORD your God is the one who goes with you. He will not fail you or forsake you." (Deuteronomy 31:6)

3. Put your hope in God.

Why are you in despair, O my soul?
And why have you become disturbed within me?
Hope in God, for I shall again praise Him
For the help of His presence. (Psalm 42:5)

4. Find rest for your soul.

"Come to Me, all who are weary and heavy-laden, and I will give you rest. Take My yoke upon you and learn from Me, for I am gentle and humble in heart, and you will find rest for your souls. For My yoke is easy and My burden is light." (Matthew 11:28–30)

5. Know that there will be a day.

And I heard a loud voice from the throne, saying, "Behold, the tabernacle of God is among men, and He will dwell among them, and they shall be His people, and God Himself will be among them, and He will wipe away every tear from their eyes; and there will no longer be any death; there will no longer be any mourning, or crying, or pain; the first things have passed away. . . . Behold, I am making all things new." (Revelation 21:3–5)

6. Don't grow weary.

Let us not lose heart in doing good, for in due time we will reap if we do not grow weary. (Galatians 6:9)

7. Trust that God cares for you.

Humble yourselves under the mighty hand of God, that He may exalt you at the proper time, casting all your anxiety on Him, because He cares for you. (1 Peter 5:6–7)

8. Believe that God heals the broken.

He heals the brokenhearted
And binds up their wounds. (Psalm 147:3)

9. Be strengthened from within.

That He would grant you, according to the riches of His glory, to be strengthened with power through His Spirit in the inner man, so that Christ may dwell in your hearts through faith. (Ephesians 3:16–17)

10. Press forward.

Brethren, I do not regard myself as having laid hold of it yet; but one thing I do: forgetting what lies behind and reaching forward to what lies ahead, I press on toward the goal for the prize of the upward call of God in Christ Jesus. (Philippians 3:13–14)

When Someone You Love Is Discouraged

Make a special effort to listen. Start by asking a few questions, and when your loved one begins to talk, don't interrupt. What he or she may need more than anything is just to process struggles verbally. He or she may vent or cry and process cyclically. Just listen. Don't try to fix the situation or make things better. Just be there. Your simplest act of kindness, your presence and concern, can make all the difference.

Actions That ATTACK
Discouragement

1. KEEP YOUR DAILY ROUTINE.

Though you may not feel like it, maintain your normal routine, heeding especially the time you get up in the morning. Don't give in to rationalizations that would keep you in bed. Get up and get out. Be with people.

2. GET MOVING.

Any physical activity will help. Poor diet and lack of exercise can make people susceptible to the blues; you can combat discouragement's spiraling effect by taking care of your body.

3. LEARN TO HANDLE ANGER AND GUILT.

Some people slide into discouragement by dwelling on past injustices or failures. Ask God to help you accept the past, forgive those who have sinned against you, and let go of your regrets (Ephesians 4:26).

4. PRACTICE THE DISCIPLINE OF GRATITUDE.

Learn to give thanks in every situation. In the back of your Bible or other convenient place, keep a running list of who and what you are thankful for.

5. FIND SUPPORT.

The comfort and perspective of others can help prevent you from spiraling deeper into discouragement. Some valleys may still be dark, but you do not have to walk through them alone.

6. CHALLENGE YOUR THINKING.

Pay attention to what you say to yourself, and don't assume it's true. Philippians 4 gives us guidelines for healthy thinking (especially verse 8)—follow them! Choosing to trust truth rather than your feelings or habitual patterns of thinking may require a lot of faith. But God will reward your efforts with peace (Philippians 4:6–7).

7. UNDERSTAND YOUR FEELINGS, BUT FOCUS ON YOUR BEHAVIOR.

Feelings are important; they are vital indicators of what's going on inside you. But it is unwise and even dangerous to base your life on them. Emotional reactions will lead to more emotional reactions, just as inappropriate thinking leads to more inappropriate thinking. Break the cycle. Do the next right thing.

8. UTILIZE THE WORD OF GOD.

Use God's Word as a resource of encouragement and power. Scripture brings perspective to the trials of life. Jesus warned that we would have problems. The apostle James echoed Him, writing that trials and temptations would come to test our faith and to teach us endurance (James 1:2–4).

Now may our Lord Jesus Christ Himself
and God our Father, who has loved us and
given us eternal comfort and good hope by
grace, comfort and strengthen your hearts
in every good work and word.
(2 Thessalonians 2:16–17)

9. SERVE OTHERS.

Intentionally turn your attention away from yourself and toward someone else. By considering how to ease someone else's pain, your own discouragement can often be reduced. Few things are better for our souls than surrounding ourselves with healthy relationships.

10. Choose healthy ways to cope with stress.

There's no "one-size-fits-all" solution, so experiment and figure out what works best for you. Resist unhealthy, self-sabotaging actions like overeating or under-eating, excessive drinking, zoning out in front of the television or computer, sleeping too much, or taking out your stress on others. Instead:

- Go for a walk.
- Call a friend.
- Sweat out tension with a good workout.
- Light scented candles.
- Listen to music.
- Savor a warm cup of coffee or tea.
- Play with a pet.
- Work at your hobby.
- Curl up with a good book.
- Watch a comedy or favorite movie.
- Write in a journal.
- Get a task out of the way (like cleaning a room in the house).

Learning how to cope with the stresses of life gives us some control over our circumstances, preventing the feelings of helplessness that so often lead to depression.

11. Lighten up!

Learn to laugh at life. The act of laughing helps your body fight stress in a number of ways. Plan into your day at least one thing you enjoy and can look forward to every day.

12. Keep short accounts.

Discover the freedom that accompanies confessing your sin to God on a daily basis (or even more often!). Also, keep the dialogue open between you and your family and close friends.

13. Play praise or worship music.

Play praise or worship music in the background as you go through your day. Turn up the music and sing in your car or in the shower.

14. REALIZE THERE IS HOPE.

You *will* feel better someday. Your hope is in God. A conviction that He is alive and in control will give you the encouragement and perspective that light the way out of the pits.

Gotta Get *Perspective* . . .
But *How*?

Stop trying to discover why. Some answers are not found this side of heaven.

Look for good, and expect to find it. Your choice of attitude will often determine what you find.

Adjust (or readjust) your lifestyle. Taking care of your physical needs is essential during down times. It affirms life and gives you the energy boost you need. Exercise regularly. Eat healthfully. Reduce caffeine and sugar. Avoid alcohol, cigarettes, and illegal drugs. Get enough sleep.

Cultivate intimacy with God. Spend time with the Lord; intentionally consider His presence with you. Believe the promise of Jeremiah 29:13: "You will seek Me and find Me when you search for Me with all your heart." Write in a journal; read the Bible. Try reading the Psalms to explore God's character. Read Proverbs every day for insight into how to live wisely. Read the Gospels to get to know Jesus better. Whatever you read, read it with the purpose of drawing closer to God. Engage in natural conversation with the Lord throughout your day.

In Time of
Questions

While in an intense season of adversity, South African pastor Andrew Murray wrote these words in his journal. Read them over and over again, and let the assurance of God's love and protection wash over you like a wave. In the time of questions say:

First, he brought me here, it is by His will I am in this strait place: in that fact I will rest.

Next, he will keep me here in His love, and give me grace to behave as His child.

Then, He will make the trial a blessing, teaching me the lessons He intends me to learn, and working in me the grace He means to bestow.

Last, in his good time He can bring me out again—how and when He knows.

Let me say I am here,
(1) By God's appointment,
(2) In His keeping,
(3) Under His training,
(4) For His time.²

REMEMBER THESE BIBLICAL PRINCIPLES

Discouragement may be a symptom of a deeper problem that needs attention (Psalm 42).

Rest and stress-relief techniques can help alleviate the gloom (Matthew 11:29).

Self-pity perpetuates the downward spiral (1 Kings 19:1–10).

Reassurance of God's power in us is a critical counter to overwhelming circumstances (2 Corinthians 4:8–11).

The Enemy of our souls can be the author of discouragement (1 Peter 5:8), and when he isn't, he is always ready to make it worse. Fight his message with all you've got, no matter what the other contributing causes may be.

A FINAL Thought

If you are suffering through a season of discouragement, see it as redemptive. It's not lost time; these aren't wasted days—a parenthesis on real living. No, this season is an experience designed to transform you, mature your faith, and move you closer to God.

In His wisdom and mercy, God uses difficult circumstances for good, despite how difficult they feel at the time. God's Spirit is at work, though you may be quite unaware of the growth that He is producing in you. He does something marvelous in you when, despite pain, you remain consistent in your desire to trust Him. You are learning patience in a world out of your control, discovering gentleness when you'd rather despair or lash out, and learning the intimate nuances of trusting God's character when your vision is blocked. Discouragement can bring tremendous depth to your relationship with God, as you surrender to His direction while traveling through a dark valley.

YOU ARE WHOLLY IN THE HANDS OF GOD

GUILT
Receiving God's Forgiveness

But I don't feel forgiven . . ."

As a follower of Christ, you might experience a time when you don't feel like your sins have been forgiven by God, no matter what others tell you or what you know to be true about His forgiveness and grace. Perhaps you think your sin is too big. Or maybe you don't think you're worthy of the pardon. Perhaps you've sinned like this before and you think that, this time, God may have drawn the line. You could read a long list of Bible verses and still not think they apply to you. To make matters worse, you may feel the subject of your sin is far too sensitive to talk about with anyone who could perhaps help.

What you know to be true in your head hasn't yet made it to your heart. You recognize that Jesus forgives the sins of those who believe in Him, but that truth hasn't yet defined your life. So, instead of feeling the freedom of the forgiveness that Jesus paid the price to provide, you're carrying around the exhausting burden of guilt. Your church sings about the wonderful grace of God, and you hold back, wondering if God has really reached you after all. You just feel guilty. And sometimes you even feel guilty for feeling guilty!

Sound familiar?

What Is Guilt? Distinguishing between Fact and Feeling

As believers in Christ, we can think of guilt in two ways. First, guilt refers to our status before God when we were unbelievers. As unforgiven sinners, we were guilty before Him, in need of a Savior. But guilt also refers to a person's response to his or her consciousness of having sinned. Before we can understand the proper place of guilt in the believer's life, we must first understand what the Bible says about our guilt before we believed.

Romans 3:23 says, "All have sinned and fall short of the glory of God." God sets His own holiness as the standard for living, and Scripture calls sin anything that falls short of that pure perfection. The apostle Paul was commenting in this verse on our status before God as unforgiven and, therefore, unrighteous sinners.

Apart from the work of Jesus Christ, we are all slaves to sin and therefore riddled with guilt through and through. This guilt separates us from God.

That's the bad news. The good news is that guilt can be resolved by our being reconnected to God through Jesus. Romans 8:1 describes the bridge that crosses the great divide between God and humanity, telling us how to know freedom from our guilty status before God: "Therefore there is now no condemnation for those who are in Christ Jesus." We go from guilty to not guilty by believing in Jesus. The unbelievable, merciful verdict from God becomes "not guilty." No separation. Those who have a relationship with Christ have no reason to fear condemnation or guilt. Jesus sets us free. (See also John 3:18.)

That said, believers continue to struggle with sin until death. And when we sin, we suffer the pangs of guilt. God has placed in every believer the convicting voice of the Holy Spirit who shows us our failure to attain God's holy standards. We feel guilt and remorse when we sin and rightly so. Our love for God and His ways compels us to do better. However, because we are forgiven believers and because Christ's righteousness covers our sin before God, guilt should not be a way of life. Instead, it should drive us to pursue repentance and seek forgiveness.

Some have never been taught the extent of the forgiveness they received when they believed in Jesus. They don't know that they've been forgiven "once for all" (1 Peter 3:18). They don't realize their "guilty feelings" may not be trustworthy. In order to live a life as full and rich as God intended, it's crucial that we understand and apply what the Bible really says about God's forgiveness and grace.

LOOK Who's *Talking*

So how can you distinguish between Satan's accusations that produce a false sense of guilt and the Spirit's conviction of actual sin? Here's a simple formula: Satan accuses in generalities; the Spirit convicts of specifics. Satan may tell you, "You're worthless; you'll never succeed in living the Christian life." The Spirit compels you to repent of something specific — "Your critical spirit toward your brother needs to change," or, "That pattern of talk is unwholesome." There is no recovery action you can take to escape Satan's accusations; he wants you to stay in the pits. The Spirit, however, gives you a way to recognize the sin, repent of it, and be released.

What the Bible Says about GOD'S *Forgiveness*

✳ WE NEED *God's Forgiveness*

Behold, the LORD's hand is not so short
That it cannot save;
Nor is His ear so dull
That it cannot hear.
But your iniquities have made a separation between you and your God,
And your sins have hidden His face from you so that He does not hear.
(Isaiah 59:1–2)

✳ TWO TYPES OF *Forgiveness*

ONCE FOR ALL	DAILY
GOD'S *forgiveness* OF OUR SIN OPENS THE DOOR TO *our salvation*.	GOD *forgives* HIS CHILDREN OF ON-GOING SINS *every time* WE ASK.
In Him we have redemption through His blood, the forgiveness of our trespasses, according to the riches of His grace. (Ephesians 1:7)	If we confess our sins, He is faithful and righteous to forgive us our sins and to cleanse us from all unrighteousness. (1 John 1:9)
Christ's sacrifice is required for our salvation.	Confession of sin is required for our fellowship with God (not our eternal salvation).
CREATES A PERMANENT RELATIONSHIP	RESTORES BROKEN FELLOWSHIP

Picture a father and daughter relationship. When the daughter rebels against the father, it doesn't end their relationship. Their fellowship is broken, however, until the daughter humbles herself and asks her father's forgiveness. When he grants it, their fellowship is restored.

What Does It Mean to Confess Our Sins?

Confession doesn't mean we beg God for forgiveness; it means we honestly agree with His opinion that specific attitudes, actions, and words are wrong. In some circles, confession of sin is a lost art, but we can only have open fellowship with God to the degree we are confessing to Him. So make sure all communication lines are open between you and God. Give Him access to your heart, and He will restore your relationship.

✳ God's Promised Results *of Forgiveness*

Happiness

Blessed [happy] is he whose transgressions are forgiven, whose sins are covered. Blessed [happy] is the man whose sin the Lord does not count against him and in whose spirit is no deceit. (Psalm 32:1–2 NIV)

No Sins Held Against Us

"I, even I, am the one who wipes out your transgressions for My own sake, And I will not remember your sins." (Isaiah 43:25)

Our Sins *Removed* from Us

As far as the east is from the west, So far has He removed our transgressions from us. (Psalm 103:12)

The Ability to *Get On* with Our Lives

Forgetting what lies behind and reaching forward to what lies ahead, I press on toward the goal for the prize of the upward call of God in Christ Jesus. (Philippians 3:13–14)

Up Close with a Personal, Forgiving Father

Look closely at 1 John 1:9. A special portrait of our loving Father appears: "If we confess our sins, he is faithful and just and will forgive us our sins and purify us from all unrighteousness" (NIV).

God "is faithful"!

That means He will forgive us every time we come to Him confessing sin. Failure to confess hinders our fellowship with God, but we will always be His children.

God is "just and will forgive us our sins."

Christ paid for all our sins — not just those we committed before our salvation!

God will "purify us from all unrighteousness."

He cleanses us from sins of which we are not even aware.

OVERCOMING
Barriers to Feeling
Forgiven

Barrier One

"What I have done is too bad. I know that God is forgiving, but I cannot be forgiven for this."

This thought implies that Christ's death was not enough to pay for all sin. We may as well say, "Maybe His atonement covers the sins of the rest of the world. But Jesus's death cannot cover *this*." This is far from the truth! Scripture declares, "Whoever will call on the name of the Lord will be saved" (Romans 10:13).

Barrier Two

"I must punish myself for my sins in order to be forgiven."

Our sins *do* deserve punishment—and Christ endured it for us. Therefore, we don't need to heap punishment upon ourselves. Personal pain adds no atoning value to Christ's sacrifice.

Barrier Three

"I know that God has forgiven me, but that doesn't matter. I cannot forgive myself."

Scripture never tells us to forgive ourselves. When we try to forgive ourselves, we attempt the impossible. Forgiveness assumes that an innocent party has been wronged, and the person who has been wronged has the job of forgiving.

God has never looked for perfect people, just faithful ones. The Bible does not describe people who have never failed but people who, when they failed, got reconnected to God and went on in faith.

21

The offending party is the one who *receives* forgiveness. We are the offender; God is the One who has been wronged, because our sin is rebellion against Him. By focusing on forgiving ourselves, we take the spotlight off God and point it at ourselves—making it doubly difficult to let go of our sin! He has forgiven us. We must simply receive His forgiveness and rest in it. Absolution from the Lord is far more powerful than absolution from oneself.

Barrier Four

"Because I am still suffering the effects of my sin, God must not have forgiven me yet."

Natural consequences do not necessarily equal God's punishment. Sins which have been forgiven long ago may still have consequences in our lives. An ex-spouse may be difficult to get along with. We may grieve on the due date of the baby that was aborted. We may suffer injuries from the accident that occurred while drinking. Yet none of these troubles represents God's punishment per se.

Barrier Five

"God has allowed too much suffering in my life; I cannot forgive God for what *He* has done."

The pain from life's losses can be devastating, and our instinctive response may be to lash out at the Sovereign One for not stopping it. The Enemy would love to keep us deceived by this mind-set of blame. God is ultimately the only truly wronged party, as He is the only One who is truly innocent (Lamentations 3:39–40). *We have sinned against Him.* In His graciousness, He has chosen to pay the penalty for our sins Himself and save us. When we are angry with the Lord, we cut ourselves off from the One who can truly heal our wounds. God is not afraid of our anger or grief; He longs to embrace us and grow us as we suffer. If you are holding on to anger against the Lord, pray for His grace to replace your pride and bitterness with humility and trust.

Godly Sorrow VS Worldly Sorrow

Godly sorrow brings repentance that leads to salvation and leaves no regret, but worldly sorrow brings death.

(2 Corinthians 7:10 NIV)

Godly sorrow leads to life, but worldly sorrow shoves us into a spiritual grave. Worldly sorrow only regrets getting caught or cries for what was lost. It never grieves for the wrong committed. When we experience godly sorrow, we are deeply grieved for the wrong we have committed. We desire to ask forgiveness, to repair the damage, to make reparation for the harm done; our desire is not merely to protect ourselves from pain or to regain what we didn't want to give up. In a word, we *repent*.

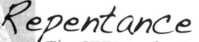

Repentance
The STEP in the Right Direction

Repentance is turning away from sin and turning back to God. This begins in the mind. When we agree with God about our sin, we are motivated to do the right thing. In our struggle through the pains of life, we must cling with all our heart to Scripture's teachings on forgiveness. Real forgiveness is available to all people—a forgiveness that satisfies our deepest longings to be cleansed inside and out. Through Christ, *all* of our sins have been paid for. God's plan is that our godly sorrow—or guilt—over our sin would cause our hearts to return to Him. He desires that we turn away from that sin, ask forgiveness—both from Him and from those we hurt—make reparation to others when possible, and then *walk on with Him*. We must let go of that sin, leaving it behind as we continue on with our Lord. As the prophet Isaiah exhorted Israel,

> "In repentance and rest you will be saved,
> In quietness and trust is your strength." (Isaiah 30:15)

Getting *past* Guilt

Go before the Lord daily in prayer.

Ask Him to reveal any sin that needs to be confessed. Then ask for His forgiveness and thank Him for it. (Note: we do not have to *keep* confessing sin that God has already forgiven.) Practice keeping short accounts with the Lord.

If you have hurt someone, if possible, *ask* this person for his or her forgiveness.

Knowing that someone is no longer holding a wrong against us is a freeing feeling, and this experience can help us understand God's forgiveness in a new way.

Write some verses about forgiveness on 3 x 5 cards and *keep* them with you.

Some good verses for this are *Psalm 103:12; Isaiah 1:18; Jeremiah 31:34; John 3:17-18; Romans 5:9-10; Romans 8:1; and 1 John 1:9.* When you struggle with guilt after you have confessed your sin, pull out your cards, and remind yourself of your true state before the Lord. Meditating on and memorizing Scripture about forgiveness and grace should be a part of your regular routine until you truly believe what God says about "no condemnation." Answer those internal false accusations with God's truth.

Not My Master Anymore

by Charles R. Swindoll

Not long ago, I had a terrific thing happen at the Dallas/Fort Worth airport. DFW is one of the reentrance portals through which our troops return home from fighting in Iraq. Near the entrance to the terminal was a small group of raw Marine recruits. They were just about to start their lives as young Marines. I stood in the background and watched their drill instructor take these guys to task! He was barking orders right and left.

I reflected on my former Marine days, more than fifty years ago. I recalled the endless harassment. This drill instructor was doing the same thing. He walked close by where I was standing and I said, "How you doing there, Sarg?" He said, "Fine, Sir, thank you." It was the first time a drill instructor ever said "sir" to me in my whole life. What a great surprise!

Why would he do that? Because I'm not his recruit. I'm not under his domination. He has no authority over me. Back in 1957, I lived at my drill instructor's mercy . . . I obeyed every word, but no longer. I could speak to the sergeant at the airport like I could anybody else. That's exactly what I must do with my "old sinful self."

Listen: you have spent long enough living under the dominating thought that you're a helpless victim of your urges and sinful drives, living as if you can't say no, living under the guilt of these repeated offenses. When, in fact, living within you is a power that exists for the purpose of giving you a whole new way of life. It's a grace-oriented lifestyle. If I have one wish for the body of Christ, it is that we would live in light of the victory we have in Christ and let the joy of grace characterize our lives rather than bowing to the frowning demands of the law!

The old nature is done getting its way. Our new nature, the one that the Spirit controls, is smoothing our path.

That happens when I stop presenting my drives, my urges, my thoughts, that which is in the innermost parts of my being, to sin as instruments of unrighteousness. You and I are not slaves to sin anymore. Instead, we

> Listen: you have spent long enough living under the dominating thought that you're a helpless victim of your urges and sinful drives . . .

present ourselves to God as those alive from the dead, and our members as instruments of righteousness to God. In other words, we deliberately and intentionally put Romans 6 into action.

We can live our lives in such a wonderful way that sin takes a backseat. Grace really unfolds when we live daily in the liberty the Spirit provides, with all the blessings of freedom that go with it. Romans 6:14 declares, "Sin shall not be master over you, for you are not under law but under grace." I like the way *The Message* paraphrase renders this: "Sin can't tell you how to live. After all, you're not living under that old tyranny any longer. You're living in the freedom of God."

Are you hearing this? Then stop the habit of obeying . . . quit saluting your former drill instructor! Sergeant Sin is no longer in charge of you.

You and I need to train ourselves to change our thinking. We've lived far too long under sin's control. Step into the brand new world Christ has designed for you and start living in the power of His Spirit.[1]

What's Happening *behind* the Scenes

After you have confessed your sin, God wants you to be assured that you are forgiven. However, Satan wants you to continue feeling guilty. The Enemy of your soul knows that your feelings of guilt keep you (in your mind) separated from God. Satan is both a deceiver and an accuser (Revelation 12:9–10).

Satan hates God and those who bear His image, and Satan is out to destroy God by destroying God's image in people. Through accusations, Satan makes us believe we are backed into a hopeless corner, a place where rescue will never come because God is as fed up with us as we are with ourselves. However, while Satan tries to make us feel guilty with his accusations, God says we are condemnation-free because Jesus paid the penalty for our sins when He died on the cross.

Because Satan cannot take away a Christian's salvation, one of his tactics is to try to take away our joy. One of his subtle strategies is to remind us of past sin. It may be something we did yesterday or years ago. It may be something we did before we came to Christ. But, when we accepted Jesus Christ as Savior, that sin was cleansed by His blood (Hebrews 9:22); God has forgotten it but Satan hasn't. If God has dismissed from His memory every sin covered by the blood of Christ (10:17), then obviously that feeling of guilt cannot come from Him. If we keep listening to Satan's accusations, our consciences will be stirred by unwarranted guilt.

How important, then, is the warning to "be of sober spirit, be on the alert. Your adversary, the devil, prowls around like a roaring lion, seeking someone to devour. But resist him, firm in your faith, knowing that the same experiences of suffering are being accomplished by your brethren who are in the world" (1 Peter 5:8–9).

How to *Live*
THE REST OF YOUR LIFE

James 3:2 says that we all fall in many ways. It's true; isn't it? No one could ever say, "Not me; I've never sinned." This entire discussion all comes down to what do you do when you're confronted with your sin? When God uses a messenger, a circumstance, or His Word to hold up a mirror to you, what do you do in that critical moment?

continued on next page

continued from previous page

You Have Several Options

You can *deny the sin* and refuse the guilt. You can say, "Well, everyone does it. I'm better than most."

You can *internalize the guilt*. "I can't believe I did that again. I stink. I'll never get victory over this area of my life!"

Or you can *own the consequences*. "I am so grieved by what I did! I hurt God. I hurt other people and myself. If I could relive it all, I would choose not to do this."

How you deal with your sin is a dividing line in how you live your life. It defines you.

What *should* you do when you realize you've sinned? Face it. Allow yourself to be broken about it. Deal with it *God's way*. Agree with Him on the severity of your actions. Ask His forgiveness, and then welcome His deepest work within you. Choose sincerity over ritual. Choose repentance over rationalization. Choose brokenness over boasting. Choose a right relationship with Him over your own pride. Choose His forgiveness over holding on to the burden of your sin.

God waits for that moment when He sees you turn around. When He sees your repentant heart, He runs to you. He lavishes you with His mercy and grace. He frees you to live an abundant life.

This could be your moment right now.

THIS COULD BE YOUR MOMENT *right now*

A FINAL Thought

Practical Bible teacher and theologian J. Dwight Pentecost summarized a believer's question regarding guilt this way:

> The child of God first of all must know and accept the facts of the doctrine that God has dismissed from His mind because of Christ's work every sin of the person who has accepted Jesus Christ as Savior. That is a fact to be believed; it is the basis of our assurance. If guilt arises, it does not originate from God. It comes from Satan who is seeking to destroy our joy. . . . Don't listen to him. Don't entertain the suggestions and doubts he puts in your mind. Instead, claim the efficacy of the blood of Christ and stand on the promise that His blood cleanses from all sin. Praise God for the blessed truth that God has affirmed that "their sins and iniquities will I remember no more." The best way to deal with Satan when he comes to make you miserable is to say bluntly, "Shut up! My sins are under the blood." If that satisfies God, it certainly ought to satisfy any one of God's children.
>
> But there can be no easing of a guilty conscience until a person comes to know Jesus Christ as his personal Savior. The truth presented here from the Word is for the benefit of God's children who may be wrestling with this problem. But it will not relieve your guilt one bit if you have never accepted Jesus Christ as Savior. You will continue to be the most miserable person in the world until you have faced this question seriously. God loves you and Christ died to save you, but you must bear your own guilt until Jesus Christ takes that guilt away by covering your sins with His blood. Accept Christ personally as your Savior now.[2]

If you would like to know more about how to begin a relationship with God, see page 47.

the Lord. We can't do life alone. For this reason, we approach God's Word to discover God's solutions to the things that distract us and keep us on edge. God's Spirit invites us to turn to the only One who offers unexplainable peace.

The *Seeds* of FEAR

Fear is a natural part of the human experience, even among Christians. It can be a healthy, God-given ability to detect and deal with danger. Like an inner warning system, healthy fear alerts us that something is wrong and prepares us to respond. A little anxiety also has its benefits. It enhances performance and competition; it strengthens concentration and spurs imagination, increasing creativity. However, when fear and anxiety are exaggerated, they become irrational and harmful. Unhealthy fear focuses on our immediate feelings and limits our ability to think clearly. Exaggerated or prolonged fear or anxiety disrupts life, drains spiritual strength, and clouds judgment.

The word translated "anxious" comes from the Greek verb meaning "to be divided or distracted." In Latin, the same word, *anxius*, carries the added nuance of choking or strangling. The word also appears in German as *wurgen*, from which we derive our English word *worry*. Anxiety threatens to strangle the life out of us, leaving us asphyxiated by fear and gasping for hope.

Jesus used the word picture of a farmer planting seeds in a field to illustrate both the nature and the destructive power of anxiety.

> "And others are the ones on whom seed was sown among the thorns; these are the ones who have heard the word, but the *worries* of the world, and the deceitfulness of riches, and the desires for other things enter in and *choke* the word, and it becomes unfruitful." (Mark 4:18–19, emphasis added)

Anxiety sprouts like weeds and thorns; it grows up around the truth of God's Word, choking away the life and peace the Word can bring.

Fear is the emotion of alarm in reaction to a perceived danger or threat. The danger may be real (the shadow of a burglar, a rapidly approaching car) or it may be imaginary (a shutter creaking in the breeze, a scary scene in a movie), but the perception is real and defined.

Anxiety is a more general, long-term feeling of uneasiness, a vague perception of threat that won't go away. It maintains the body at a low-level of alertness. While fear brings a rush of adrenaline, anxiety is a slow drip. When alertness is called for, this ready-to-react anxiety can provide energy and creativity, but over the long haul, it puts a strain on both mind and body.

Worry is not an emotion; it is the mental action of bringing up conflicts or fears, mulling over them, and contemplating worst-case scenarios. This reaction to anxiety increases anxiety. Worry is an unproductive form of problem-solving because it is applied to things that can't be changed or avoided by wishing.

In order to conquer anxiety, our lives need a continuous inner climate of confidence in God. God's Spirit, when we allow Him freedom to move in our hearts, produces a change in our character. When He does, fear can be replaced with confidence. In 2 Timothy 1:7, Paul suggested three substitutes:

POWER—
the inexhaustible energy and competence that comes from God

LOVE—
the unfearing, sacrificial love that focuses on others rather than ourselves

DISCIPLINE—
self-discipline that yields wise, productive thinking

From Genesis to Revelation, Scripture is packed with examples, stories, and wisdom drawn from circumstances that have driven people to the edges of cliffs. Again and again, God calls people to trust Him and place their hope for life and peace in His hands.

* *Adam* AND *Eve*

When Adam and Eve threw open the door to sin, fear rushed in too. Before they sinned, they had known intimate, open communication with God. The only fear they could have known was the reverent, submissive awe of God's presence that is the beginning of wisdom (Psalm 111:10; Proverbs 1:7; 9:10; Isaiah 33:6). But when they tried to take their lives and destinies out of God's hands, they immediately felt naked, vulnerable, ashamed, and unprotected. They felt fear, and so they hid from God.

This biblical example gives us valuable insight into our problems with fear and anxiety. Significant, ongoing problems with fear and anxiety are complicated by our sinful nature, which escalates our worries, steals our peace of mind, and influences us to make wrong choices. When operating in fear:

- We hide, isolating ourselves from God's help, though freedom is found in the light of His presence.

- We try to solve our problems by self-reliance and end up self-condemned.

- We multiply our anxieties through fear of God's judgment and thereby close ourselves off from His restoring love and transforming strength.

✳ THE *Children* OF *Israel*

The children of Israel emerged from centuries of slavery to become a new, free nation under Moses. They were accustomed to the anxiety that powerlessness breeds. As they faced their enemies on the path toward the Promised Land, God called them to put aside fear and have faith in His powerful intervention on their behalf:

- "Do not fear! Stand by and see the salvation of the LORD which He will accomplish for you today" (Exodus 14:13).

- "Do not fear them, for the LORD your God is the one fighting for you" (Deuteronomy 3:22).

- "Do not fear them, for I have given them into your hands" (Joshua 10:8).

Anxiety, then, is evidence that we really don't expect God to intervene in our lives to accomplish His purposes and meet our needs.

Anxiety may stem from unconscious feelings. But worry is a conscious act of choosing an ineffective method of coping with life. Worry actually implies the absence of trust in God. And because Scripture instructs us NOT to worry, this lack of trust in God is certainly sin (see Matthew 6:34).

✳ *King David*

David, the shepherd-king, poet, and man after God's own heart, was thoroughly acquainted with paralyzing fear and constant anxiety. During the years he spent on the run from the murderous Saul, David learned to turn to God for reassurance. The psalms David wrote during this season teach us that danger and pain must drive us *to* God, not *from* Him. We also learn from David to release the power of our emotions toward God and to think of God and our lives rightly by focusing on *His* power and love:

- "The LORD is my rock and my fortress and my deliverer,
  My God, my rock, in whom I take refuge;
  My shield and the horn of my salvation, my stronghold.
  I call upon the LORD, who is worthy to be praised,
  And I am saved from my enemies" (Psalm 18:2–3).

- "The LORD is my shepherd,
  I shall not want. . . .
  I fear no evil, for You are with me;
  Your rod and Your staff, they comfort me" (23:1, 4).

- "The LORD is my light and my salvation;
  Whom shall I fear?
  The LORD is the defense of my life;
  Whom shall I dread?" (27:1).

- "He who dwells in the shelter of the Most High
  Will abide in the shadow of the Almighty. . . .
  He will cover you with His pinions,
  And under His wings you may seek refuge" (91:1, 4).

What we need most when we encounter fearful circumstances is perspective. A healthy fear of God puts our greatest fears in proper priority. When we are stripped of hope as we encounter sickness, accidents, or any long list of life's difficult circumstances, nothing can put our thinking in better perspective than a clear view of the face of God.

✳ Proverbs

The book of Proverbs teaches us to overcome anxiety by fearing the Lord and only Him:

- "He who fears the LORD has a secure fortress,
  and for his children it will be a refuge" (Proverbs 14:26 NIV).

- "The fear of the LORD leads to life:
  Then one rests content, untouched by trouble" (19:23 NIV).

STRONG Words FROM SCRIPTURE

Direct your energy toward your true source of hope.
—Psalm 9:9–10; Romans 5:3–5

Stop worrying and start praying.—Psalm 34:1–4; Philippians 4:6–9

Replace fretting with trust.—Psalm 37

Center your thoughts on God, not on worry.—Isaiah 26:3

Choose not to worry; it doesn't work.—Matthew 6:25–34

Focus on the solution, not the problem.—Matthew 14:22–33

Give God your worry in advance.—1 Peter 5:6–7

* Isaiah

The prophet Isaiah prepared the people of God for the most fearful of times: the years that would bring the destruction of the nation and their captivity in Babylon. In the midst of the storm, they would need to cling to God's reassurances of His loving choice of them . . . or be swept away by their own anxieties:

- "For I am the LORD your God, who upholds your right hand,
  Who says to you, 'Do not fear, I will help you'" (Isaiah 41:13).

- "Do not fear, for I have redeemed you; I have called you by name; you are Mine!" (43:1).

- "Thus says the LORD who made you
  And formed you in the womb, who will help you,
  'Do not fear, O Jacob My servant;
  And you Jeshurun whom I have chosen'" (44:2).

Our Lord Jesus gives us
a legacy of peace

"Peace I leave with you; My peace I give to you; not as the world gives do I give to you. Do not let your heart be troubled, nor let it be fearful." (John 14:27)

<small>CHRIST'S TWO CHARACTERISTIC PHRASES OF REASSURANCE AND COMMAND ARE:</small>

"Don't be afraid; just believe" (Mark 5:36 NIV) and, "Take courage; it is I, do not be afraid" (6:50).

* Jesus

Jesus thought worry an important enough topic that He addressed it in His Sermon on the Mount. Here's what He said:

- Worry is *unreasonable*. "Is not life more than food, and the body more than clothing?" (Matthew 6:25).

- Worry is *unnatural*. "Look at the birds of the air . . . your heavenly Father feeds them" (6:26).

- Worry is *unhelpful*. "Who of you by being worried can add a single hour to his life?" (6:27).

- Worry is *unnecessary*. "Will he not . . . clothe you?" (6:30 NIV).

Prayer Makes All the DIFFERENCE

Hardship and difficulties are indispensable parts of God's process of bringing His people to spiritual maturity. When we come to realize this and accept it, we will be less inclined to panic when the next problem appears on the horizon. We will instead say to ourselves, "Aha, so this is the next learning experience in God's curriculum for me!"

Be *Anxious* for Nothing

> Be anxious for nothing, but in everything by prayer and supplication with thanksgiving let your requests be made known to God. And the peace of God, which surpasses all comprehension, will guard your hearts and your minds in Christ Jesus. Finally, brethren, whatever is true, whatever is honorable, whatever is right, whatever is pure, whatever is lovely, whatever is of good repute, if there is any excellence and if anything worthy of praise, dwell on these things. The things you have learned and received and heard and seen in me, practice these things, and the God of peace will be with you. (Philippians 4:6–9)

When you feel anxious, God's Word reveals three things you can do and one promise if you do them.

1. Go to God in PRAYER. *Prayer* is communicating with God as your Father with a sense of worship, reverence, and awe. When you're anxious, make a choice to worship God.

2. Take your REQUESTS to God. Be honest. Tell the Lord your need and your deep desire for that need to be met.

3. Always go to God with an attitude of GRATITUDE. Thank the Lord for hearing you. Thank Him for how He's cared for you in the past and for how He will again, even if you can't guess how.

God promises to exchange your worries for an unexplainable peace that will guard both your heart and your mind. His peace will act as a company of soldiers to protect and defend you in your weak moments.

Three Promises to Help You Pray

by Charles R. Swindoll

one
GOD PROMISES THAT HE WILL HEAR AND ANSWER, REGARDLESS OF THE HOUR

> *And how bold and free we then become in his presence, freely asking according to his will, sure that he's listening. And if we're confident that he's listening, we know that what we've asked for is as good as ours.*
> (1 John 5:14–15 MSG)

God is never too busy. He never sleeps. He never has His mind so occupied with running the universe that He will not hear you. And yet, never forget that an answer to prayer doesn't mean that He will solve our problems the way we want them solved. He will hear our requests and respond with solutions—sometimes surprising ones—that not only address our concerns but deepen our faith in His wisdom and strengthen our confidence in His sovereignty.

two
GOD PROMISES HIS PRESENCE, REGARDLESS OF THE OUTCOME

God wants good things for every son and daughter, and He wants to bless us but never at the expense of our holiness. He may choose to deny our request for one blessing if the refusal paves the way for a greater one.

Paul, no doubt, was terribly disappointed and frustrated when God refused his reasonable request for relief from excruciating pain (see 2 Corinthians 12:7–10).

In time, Paul discovered that God had given him something greater than relief from pain. God denied what Paul wanted in favor of what Paul needed—a greater sense of God's presence. Paul shared this painful story with his Christian disciples in Corinth to assure them that God will do the same for all believers. That includes you.

three

Remember the outcome God promised as a result of continual prayer?

> *Before you know it, a sense of God's wholeness, everything coming together for good, will come and settle you down. It's wonderful what happens when Christ displaces worry at the center of your life.*
> (Philippians 4:7 MSG)

What does the Lord provide in place of worry? A deep and abiding peace. A tranquility that others can't understand. They'll look at you, calm in the middle of a raging storm that life has rained down on you, and they will say, "How can you possibly be calm at a time like this?" And your answer will be, "I have no idea—except to say that my hope is in the Lord. God is good, He is in control, and in the end I will be fine." Few thoughts bring greater comfort.

God's goal for us is intimacy with Him. I have discovered, however, that the cultivation of intimacy can get complicated. That happens when our will gets in the way of seeking His.

Our primary goal in calling out to God throughout a life of prayer is not to make our daily existence easier for ourselves—although, from a certain point of view, it will. Life's primary goal can be summed up in four words: *intimacy with the Almighty.* Seek that first, and you will have everything you've longed for in life, including all the things you never knew you needed.[1]

Critical Weapons for *Fighting Anxiety*

Courage (Psalm 31:24)

Stability (Psalm 62)

Perspective (Romans 5:2–5)

Comfort (2 Corinthians 1:3–7)

Hope (1 John 3:1–3)

Prerequisites for Peace from John 14

First: depend upon the person of the Holy Spirit (John 14:25–26).

When you're given to fear, you forget the truth you thought you knew. When you're depending on God's Spirit, He reminds you of God's truth at the exact moment you need it.

Second: claim the peace of Jesus Christ (14:27).

The way of thinking we've learned from the world offers no lasting peace. When you depend on the Lord, He delivers deep-seated, internal confidence in His ability to rescue and restore you.

Third: accept God's plan for the future (14:28).

The Father's plan is not an "if" plan, it's a "when" plan. The arrangement that the Father has laid out for the future events in your life and in the world at large is clearly defined and controlled by Him.

Fourth: follow the pattern of obedience (14:30–31).

Jesus said, "I'm carrying out My Father's plan." You will never know peace in a life of disobedience. Do you know the next step to take? Then do that. Follow the Lord's pattern of obedience.

A WORD FROM CHUCK
Replace Anxiety with Contentment

When Christ becomes our central focus, our reason for existence, contentment replaces our anxiety as well as our fears and insecurities. How does He do it?

1. *He broadens the dimensions of our circumstances*. This gives us new confidence. Chains that once bound and irritated us no longer seem irksome. Our limitations become challenges rather than chores.

2. *He delivers us from preoccupation with others*. This causes our contentment level to rise. Other people's opinions, motives, and criticisms no longer seem all that important. What a wonderful deliverance!

3. *He calms our fears regarding ourselves and our future*. This provides a burst of fresh hope on a daily basis. Once fear is removed, it is remarkable how quickly peace fills the vacuum.

And when we get those three ducks in a row, it isn't long before we begin to laugh again. What a way to live! Let me urge you not to let anything keep you from it.[2]

Homework

Memorize key passages to help you deal with fear, anxiety, and worry, beginning with *Psalm 121*. Personalize these Scripture passages as you memorize them. (The following list will give you a good place to go after Psalm 121.)

☐ *Deuteronomy 31:8* ☐ *Matthew 6:25-34*

☐ *Psalm 23; 25; 103* ☐ *Philippians 4:6-9*

☐ *Proverbs 3:5-8* ☐ *2 Timothy 1:7*

☐ *Isaiah 27:3-4* ☐ *Hebrews 13:5-6*

A FINAL Thought

God doesn't want us to compartmentalize our lives. He wants every aspect to be surrendered to His control. Selective trust makes us forget His everyday provisions. The less we allow Him to be part of our everyday lives, the more anxious we become. How easy it is to tell ourselves that *this* is in the realm of God's concern but not *that*. Wrong! Dividing life into sacred and secular categories makes us forget His goodness. Dividing makes us forgetful.

Reflect on your list of worries. Take a good look through the current events of your life. What is causing you to be anxious? Overcoming those fears won't be easy. Simply sitting in a church service or finding some magical Bible verse won't work. You probably already know that. It will take time and perseverance. But the truth is, no matter what you are facing, worrying will do you more harm than good.

Eugene Peterson has captured Jesus's words in today's terms. Please read them slowly and aloud. Let them sink in softly and thoughtfully.

> "Look at the birds, free and unfettered, not tied down to a job description, careless in the care of God. And you count far more to him than birds. . . . What I'm trying to do here is to get you to relax, to not be so preoccupied with *getting*, so you can respond to God's *giving*. People who don't know God and the way he works fuss over these things, but you know both God and how he works. Steep your life in God-reality, God-initiative, God-provisions. Don't worry about missing out. You'll find all your everyday human concerns will be met. Give your entire attention to what God is

doing right now, and don't get worked up about what may or may not happen tomorrow. God will help you deal with whatever hard things come up when the time comes." (Matthew 6:26, 31–34 MSG)

How to Begin a Relationship with God

Are you facing difficult days? They may be the best thing that's ever happened to you!

Here's why: God often uses difficult circumstances to reveal our need for Him. If life was smooth and carefree, we would think we could handle it on our own. Nothing could be further from the truth. The truth is: you need God.

The burdens of discouragement, guilt, and anxiety lift with the realization that Jesus's death on the cross paid the complete price for your sins. The Bible says that while we were still sinners, Christ died for us. If this is new information to you, please keep reading. See past the pain of this moment to the reality that there is nothing you need to do or become in order to be accepted by God. Just simply trust in Jesus. You'll discover the best news you've ever heard. We've listed it below as four essential truths. Let's look at each in detail.

Our Spiritual Condition: Totally Depraved

The first truth is rather personal. One look in the mirror of Scripture, and our human condition becomes painfully clear:

> "There is none righteous, not even one;
> There is none who understands,
> There is none who seeks for God;
> All have turned aside, together they have become
>   useless;
> There is none who does good,
> There is not even one." (Romans 3:10–12)

We are all sinners through and through—totally depraved. Now, that doesn't mean we've committed every atrocity known to humankind.

We're not as *bad* as we can be, just as *bad off* as we can be. Sin colors all our thoughts, motives, words, and actions.

If you've been around a while, you likely already believe it. Look around. Everything around us bears the smudge marks of our sinful nature. Despite our best efforts to create a perfect world, crime statistics continue to soar, divorce rates keep climbing, and families keep crumbling.

Something has gone terribly wrong in our society and in ourselves—something deadly. Contrary to how the world would repackage it, "me-first" living doesn't equal rugged individuality and freedom; it equals death. As Paul said in his letter to the Romans, "The wages of sin is death" (Romans 6:23)—our spiritual and physical death that comes from God's righteous judgment of our sin, along with all of the emotional and practical effects of this separation that we experience on a daily basis. This brings us to the second marker: God's character.

God's Character: Infinitely Holy

How can God judge us for a sinful state we were born into? Our total depravity is only half the answer. The other half is God's infinite holiness.

The fact that we know things are not as they should be points us to a standard of goodness beyond ourselves. Our sense of injustice in life on this side of eternity implies a perfect standard of justice beyond our reality. That standard and source is God Himself. And God's standard of holiness contrasts starkly with our sinful condition.

Scripture says that "God is Light, and in Him there is no darkness at all" (1 John 1:5). God is absolutely holy—which creates a problem for us. If He is so pure, how can we who are so impure relate to Him?

Perhaps we could try being better people, try to tilt the balance in favor of our good deeds, or seek out methods for self-improvement. Throughout history, people have attempted to live up to God's standard by keeping the Ten Commandments or living by their own code of ethics. Unfortunately, no one can come close to satisfying the demands of God's law. Romans 3:20 says, "By the works of the Law no flesh will be justified in His sight; for through the Law comes the knowledge of sin."

Our Need: A Substitute

So here we are, sinners by nature and sinners by choice, trying to pull ourselves up by our own bootstraps to attain a relationship with our holy Creator. But every time we try, we fall flat on our faces. We can't live a good enough life to make up for our sin, because God's standard isn't "good enough"—it's *perfection*. And we can't make amends for the offense our sin has created without dying for it.

Who can get us out of this mess?

If someone could live perfectly, honoring God's law, and would bear sin's death penalty for us—in our place—then we would be saved from our predicament. But is there such a person? Thankfully, yes!

Meet your substitute—*Jesus Christ*. He is the One who took death's place for you!

> [God] made [Jesus Christ] who knew no sin to be sin on our behalf, so that we might become the righteousness of God in Him. (2 Corinthians 5:21)

God's Provision: A Savior

God rescued us by sending His Son, Jesus, to die on the cross for our sins (1 John 4:9–10). Jesus was fully human and fully divine (John 1:1, 18), a truth that ensures His understanding of our weaknesses, His power to forgive, and His ability to bridge the gap between God and us (Romans 5:6–11). In short, we are "justified as a gift by His grace through the redemption which is in Christ Jesus" (Romans 3:24). Two words in this verse bear further explanation: *justified* and *redemption*.

Justification is God's act of mercy, in which He declares righteous the believing sinners while we are still in our sinning state. Justification doesn't mean that God *makes* us righteous, so that we never sin again, rather that He *declares* us righteous—much like a judge pardons a guilty criminal. Because Jesus took our sin upon Himself and suffered our judgment on the cross, God forgives our debt and proclaims us PARDONED.

Redemption is Christ's act of paying the complete price to release us from sin's bondage. God sent His Son to bear His wrath for all of our sins—past, present, and future (Romans 3:24–26; 2 Corinthians 5:21). In humble obedience, Christ willingly endured the shame of the cross for our sake (Mark 10:45; Romans 5:6–8; Philippians 2:8). Christ's death satisfied God's righteous demands. He no longer holds our sins against us, because His own Son paid the penalty for them. We are freed from the slave market of sin, never to be enslaved again!

Placing Your Faith in Christ

These four truths describe how God has provided a way to Himself through Jesus Christ. Because the price has been paid in full by God, we must respond to His free gift of eternal life in total faith and confidence in Him to save us. We must step forward into the relationship with God that He has prepared for us—not by doing good works or by being a good person, but by coming to Him just as we are and accepting His justification and redemption by faith..

> For by grace you have been saved through faith; and that not of yourselves, it is the gift of God; not as a result of works, so that no one may boast. (Ephesians 2:8–9)

We accept God's gift of salvation simply by placing our faith in Christ alone for the forgiveness of our sins. Would you like to enter a relationship with your Creator by trusting in Christ as your Savior? If so, here's a simple prayer you can use to express your faith:

> *Dear God,*
>
> *I know that my sin has put a barrier between You and me. Thank You for sending Your Son, Jesus, to die in my place. I trust in Jesus alone to forgive my sins, and I accept His gift of eternal life. I ask Jesus to be my personal Savior and the Lord of my life. Thank You. In Jesus's name, amen.*

If you've prayed this prayer or one like it and you wish to find out more about knowing God and His plan for you in the Bible, contact us at Insight for Living. Our contact information is on the following pages.

We Are Here for You

If you desire to find out more about knowing God and His plan for you in the Bible, contact us. Insight for Living provides staff pastors who are available for free written correspondence or phone consultation. These seminary-trained and seasoned counselors have years of experience and are well-qualified guides for your spiritual journey.

Please feel welcome to contact your regional Pastoral Ministries by using the information below:

United States
Insight for Living
Pastoral Ministries
Post Office Box 269000
Plano, Texas 75026-9000
USA
972-473-5097, Monday through Friday,
8:00 a.m. – 5:00 p.m. central time
www.insight.org/contactapastor

Canada
Insight for Living Canada
Pastoral Ministries
Post Office Box 2510
Vancouver, BC V6B 3W7
CANADA
1-800-663-7639
info@insightforliving.ca

Australia, New Zealand, and South Pacific
Insight for Living Australia
Pastoral Care
Post Office Box 443
Boronia, VIC 3155
AUSTRALIA
1300 467 444

United Kingdom and Europe
Insight for Living United Kingdom
Pastoral Care
PO Box 553
Dorking
RH4 9EU
UNITED KINGDOM
0800 915 9364
+44 (0)1306 640156
pastoralcare@insightforliving.org.uk

Endnotes

Chapter 1
Discouragement: Getting to the Other Side

1. Adapted from Charles R. Swindoll, *Living above the Level of Mediocrity: A Commitment to Excellence* (Dallas: Word, 1989), 240–43.

2. Andrew Murray, as quoted in V. Raymond Edmond, *They Found the Secret: 20 Transformed Lives that Reveal a Touch of Eternity* (Grand Rapids: Zondervan, 1984), 117–18.

Chapter 2
Guilt: Receiving God's Forgiveness

1. Adapted from Charles R. Swindoll, *Embraced by the Spirit: The Untold Blessing of Intimacy with God* (Grand Rapids: Zondervan, 2010), 134–38.

2. J. Dwight Pentecost, *Man's Problems — God's Answers* (Chicago: Moody Press, 1972), 22–23.

Chapter 3
Anxiety: Transforming Fear into Faith

1. Adapted from Charles R. Swindoll, *The Owner's Manual for Christians: The Essential Guide for a God-Honoring Life* (Nashville: Thomas Nelson, 2009), 100–102.

2. Adapted from Charles R. Swindoll, *Laugh Again* (Dallas: Word, 1991), 57–58.

Recommended Resources
from Charles R. Swindoll
and Insight for Living

Books

Swindoll, Charles R. *Encouragement for Life: Words of Hope and Inspiration.* Nashville: J. Countryman, 2006.

Swindoll, Charles R. *Getting Through the Tough Stuff: It's Always Something!* Nashville: W Publishing, 2004.

Swindoll, Charles R. *The Owner's Manual for Christians: The Essential Guide for a God-Honoring Life.* Nashville: Thomas Nelson, 2009.

Booklets

Swindoll, Charles R. *How Can I Win Over Worry?* Plano, Tex.: IFL Publishing House, 2009.

Swindoll, Charles R. *Overcoming Anxiety.* Plano, Tex.: IFL Publishing House, 2008.

Messages on CD

Swindoll, Charles R. "Discouragement: Its Causes and Cure." In *Hand Me Another Brick.* Plano, Tex.: Insight for Living, 1974. Compact disc.

Swindoll, Charles R. "Encouragement Served Family Style." In *Growing Deep in the Christian Life.* Plano, Tex.: Insight for Living, 1984. Compact disc.

Swindoll, Charles R. "Getting Past the Guilt of Your Past." In *Family Matters.* Plano, Tex.: Insight for Living, 2010. Compact disc.*

Swindoll, Charles R. "God's Peace in Philippians 4." In *Meeting God in Familiar Places.* Plano, Tex.: Insight for Living, 2008. Compact disc.*

Series on CD

Swindoll, Charles R. *Character Counts: Building a Life That Pleases God.* Plano, Tex.: Insight for Living, 2008. 12 compact discs.*

Swindoll, Charles R. *Getting Through the Tough Stuff: It's Always Something!* Plano, Tex.: Insight for Living, 2010. 14 compact discs.*

Swindoll, Charles R. *Issues and Answers in Jesus's Day.* Plano, Tex.: Insight for Living, 1989. 18 compact discs.

* Available also in MP3 format

Ordering Information

If you would like to order additional copies of *The Secret to Facing Hard Days: Insight on Discouragement, Guilt, and Anxiety* or to order other Insight for Living resources, please contact the office that serves you.

United States
Insight for Living
Post Office Box 269000
Plano, Texas 75026-9000
USA
1-800-772-8888 (Monday through Friday,
7:00 a.m.–7:00 p.m. central time)
www.insight.org
www.insightworld.org

Canada
Insight for Living Canada
Post Office Box 2510
Vancouver, BC V6B 3W7
CANADA
1-800-663-7639
www.insightforliving.ca

Australia, New Zealand, and South Pacific
Insight for Living Australia
Post Office Box 443
Boronia, VIC 3155
AUSTRALIA
1300 467 444
www.insight.asn.au

United Kingdom and Europe
Insight for Living United Kingdom
PO Box 553
Dorking
RH4 9EU
UNITED KINGDOM
0800 915 9364
www.insightforliving.org.uk

Other International Locations
International constituents may contact the U.S. office through our Web site (www.insightworld.org), mail queries, or by calling +1-972-473-5136.